Sasha Mullen & Lexi Rees
Art by Eveyjoan

BE MORE YOU

Fun mindfulness activities and tools you can use every day!

Published in Great Britain
By Outset Publishing Ltd

First edition published July 2022

Written by Sasha Mullen and Lexi Rees
Illustration and Design by Eveyjoan

Copyright © Sasha Mullen and Lexi Rees 2021

Sasha Mullen and Lexi Rees have asserted their rights under the Copyright, Designs and Patents Act 1988 to be identified as the authors of this work.

All rights reserved. No part of this publication may be reproduced, stored in a retrieval system, or transmitted, in any form or by any means, without the prior permission in writing of the publisher, nor be otherwise circulated in any form of binding or cover other than that in which it is published and without a similar condition including this condition being imposed on the subsequent purchaser.

ISBN: 978-1-913799-14-4

www.lexirees.co.uk
www.themindfulmentors.com

IT'S OFFICIAL, YOU ARE AMAZING!

Everybody has moments when they don't feel amazing inside. We might be sad or angry or frustrated, or there could even be lots of emotions all jumbled up inside us. It can be difficult when this happens, but the good news is there are lots of things we can do to help our minds process these emotions.

Through this journal, you're going to build your very own mindfulness <u>tool kit</u>. Every chapter you complete unlocks awesome new skills. By the time you finish all the activities, you'll know how to do all these things:

- Be kind to yourself and others
- Tackle your worries
- Stay focused
- Boost your self esteem
- Control your instincts
- Manage your emotions
- Find inner peace

With these tools, you can be your most amazing self every day.

Look out for this icon as you go through the book.

How To Use This Journal

The journal is divided into sections. Each section builds a set of skills through several different activities. Just like you might train for a sport or learn how to play a musical instrument, the activities in each section are designed to help you practise these skills so you can get really good at them.

You can work through most of the sections in order or, if there are areas that are worrying you at the moment, you might like to turn to those sections and start there.

By practising mindfulness and building your tool kit, you can take control of your mind and body.

→ **Be** More **You!**

Activity Key
- Science
- Art
- Visualisation
- Game
- Analysis
- To do
- Breathing

Keep an eye out for these tips throughout this journal!

MINDFUL MAGIC

When you use this tool kit, you're practising "mindfulness". Mindfulness helps you to accept things as they are. There's no judgement or criticism, just understanding.

CONTENTS

1. Keep your Balance

2. Sort Fact from Fiction

3. Boost your Confidence

4. Identify your Emotions

5. Master your Instincts

6. Change your Weather

7. Pay it Forward

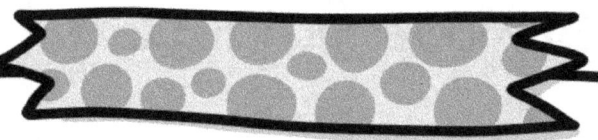

This journal belongs to:

. . . .

Chapter 1

Keep Your Balance

In this chapter we're going to:

- Surround yourself with supportive people
- Balance your everyday activities
- Tackle your worries

Before we start, check in with yourself. How are you feeling?

My body feels: hot/ fuzzy/ tingly/ still / itchy/ heavy/ light

My mind feels: excited/ upset/ angry/ happy/ calm/ exhausted

MINDFUL MAGIC

Can you see connections between your body sensations and your feelings? E.g. when my body is heavy, I feel tired, when my body is light as a feather, I feel happy.

 # BRAIN SCIENCE RECAP

If you've read BElieve in YOurself, you'll have seen lots about the four parts of the brain, and what they do. When they work together, you get amazing results.

Let's start with a quick recap.

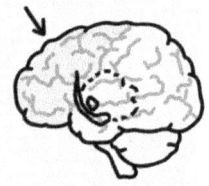 Pre frontal Cortex = Focus Function

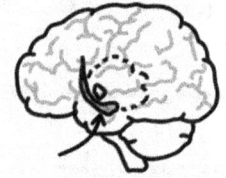 Hippocampus = Record Keeper

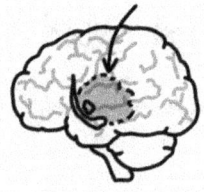 Insula = Emotions Radar

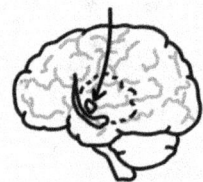 Amygdala = Survival Instinct

Don't Panic!
This page is beautifully blank.

WAVE RIDER

When you have an unwanted emotion, try riding it like a surfboarder on a wave. Don't forget, every wave eventually ends up on the beach.

1. Close your eyes and acknowledge the emotion.

2. Imagine it as a wave building in front of you. Point your finger at the wave.

3. Take a deep breath in and let your finger ride the wave, tracing it all the way to the crest.

4. Breathe out, making a 'shhhhh' sound, and trace the fall of the wave down with your finger until it's just a gentle splash on the beach.

5. Repeat this **four** more times.

How do you feel now?

. . . .

Seesaw Skills

Think about all the activities you do in a week. Make a list of all things you enjoy on one side of the seesaw and all the ones you're less fond of on the other side.

How balanced is your seesaw?

....
....
....
....
....
....

....
....
....
....
....

After doing an activity you don't enjoy much, balance the seesaw by doing something you love.

MINDFUL MAGIC

When activities make you sad or frustrated, let your "emotions radar" (insula) recognise it's only a temporary feeling. Try using a breathing technique to calm your mind.

Confidence Cube

Positive words to describe me are ...

I am really good at ...

I love ...

My biggest achievements are ...

I am proud of ...

I am confident when ...

1. Cut out this shape.
2. Glue or tape the tabs to make a dice.
3. Roll the dice and think of that many answers to finish the sentence.

It can be difficult to decide what our strengths are. If you're stuck, ask your friends and family for ideas.

I'm too cool
to be square!

Worry Jar

Everyone has worries.

- Find an old jam jar with a lid.
- Write or draw your worries on scraps of paper and seal them in the jar.
- Whenever you have a new worry, you can add it to the jar.
- This helps stop them from cluttering up your mind so you can focus on other things.
- Once a week, take out the jar and read your notes. Throw away any that are no longer worrying you.

Fill the jar clear your head

MINDFUL MAGIC

One day, you may discover there are fewer worries in your jar. This is great! It means you've been using your mindfulness tools effectively, perhaps without even noticing.

Be A Tree

Tree pose is a famous yoga move. It requires balance and co-ordination, and you'll have to use your "focus function" (pre-frontal cortex). A good time to try this activity is before you start a task you need to concentrate on, like your homework.

This activity is easier if you wear loose, comfortable clothing.

1. Find a quiet and spacious place.
2. Stand with your feet shoulder width apart, arms by your side.
3. As you breathe in, raise your hands above your head. Keep your arms straight like tree branches.
4. Hold that pose as you breathe out.
5. With the next breath in, lift one foot of the floor and place the sole of your foot on your calf.
6. Breathe out.
7. Breathe in and begin to wiggle your foot up towards the knee or thigh, wherever feels comfortable.

8. Keep your balance and take three slow breaths here.

9. Lower your arms and foot at the same time.

10. Repeat with the other leg, raising your arms first and then your foot.

11. Once you're in the final pose, take three deep breaths.

12. Gently lower your arms and foot.

How do you feel now? Circle the word/s or add your own feeling.

focused　　　calm　　　happy　　　balanced　　　_____

MINDFUL MAGIC

Well done! You've achieved a deep state of calmness and balance. For an extra challenge, try this with closed eyes.

CONGRATULATIONS!

You have just unlocked the first three mindfulness tools for your toolbox! These help you to accept all your feelings and find ways to overcome them.

In the Toolbox:

 Ride those Waves like a professional surfer.

 Seal your worries away in the Worry Jar.

 Grow roots like a Tree to steady yourself.

You are now ready to use these tools anywhere!

Chapter 2

Sort Fact from Fiction

In this chapter we're going to:

- sort thoughts from facts
- Let go of unwanted thoughts
- Focus on your goals

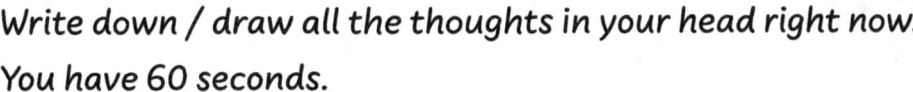

Before we start, check in with yourself. What are you thinking right now?

Write down / draw all the thoughts in your head right now.
You have 60 seconds.

How do these thoughts make you feel?

The Focus Function

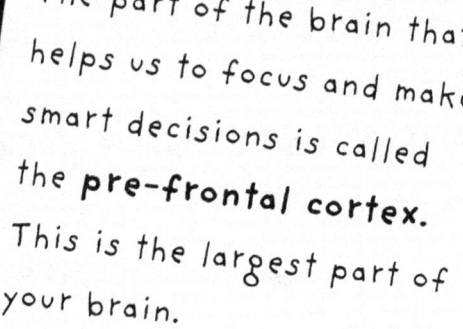

The part of the brain that helps us to focus and make smart decisions is called the **pre-frontal cortex**. This is the largest part of your brain.

Prefrontal cortex

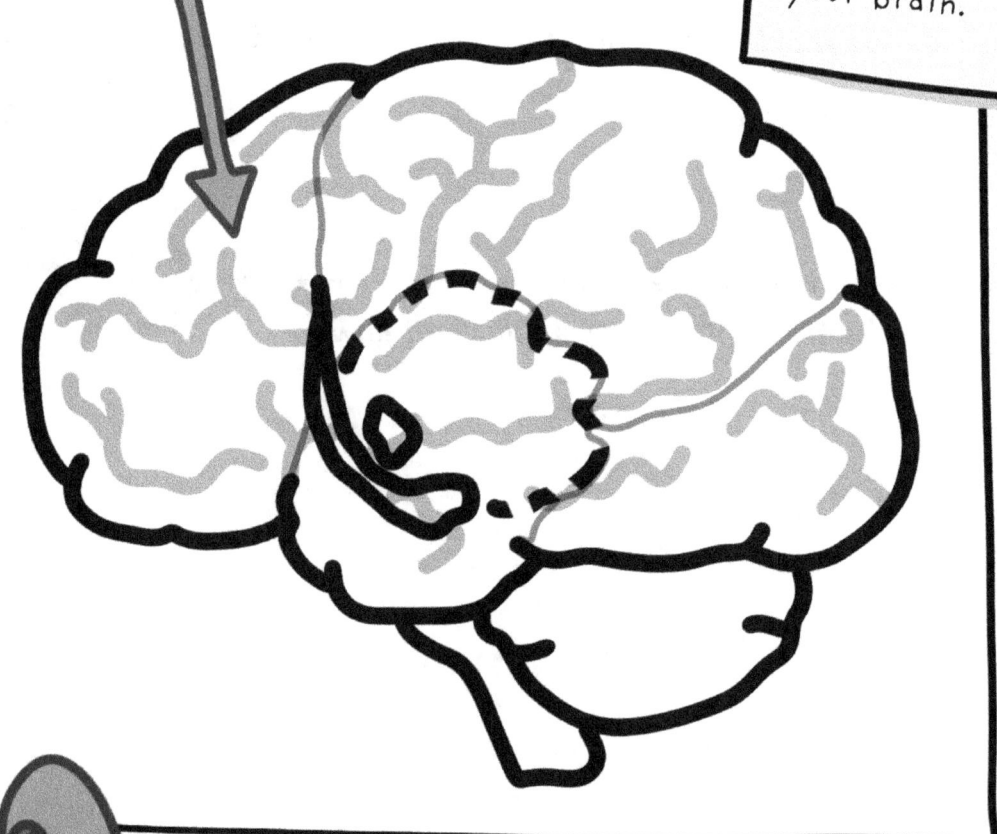

The pre-frontal cortex follows this formula:

Stay focused + Make good decisions   =   Be your calmest self

WAVES OF POSITIVITY

In each wave, write something positive about YOUrself and colour it in.

Stick this page somewhere you can see it.

I am brilliant at ...

I enjoy ...

I have ...

I'm a surfing superstar

Drift Away

Some thoughts bring unwanted feelings. Remind yourself that these are just thoughts, they are not real, and they will go away. When this happens, think of Winnie the Pooh's favourite game of Pooh Sticks and try this activity.

1. Find somewhere comfortable to sit or lie down.
2. Close your eyes.
3. Visualise a beautiful valley with a sparkling river running through it.
4. Breathe in the cool, crisp air.
5. Picture your negative thoughts as sticks and throw them into the stream.
6. Let the current carry the sticks away down the river, leaving your mind as clear as the water.
7. Breathe out.
8. Repeat this until all your unwanted thoughts have drifted away.
9. Open your eyes and smile.

What are **you** thinking about now?

....

....

If you still have unwanted thoughts, try the visualisation again.

MINDFUL MAGIC
As well as helping to control unwanted thoughts, this frees up space in your head for positive thoughts.

FACT OR FICTION SORTER

Draw a line from each statement to the correct box.

Being hit by a snowball can hurt.
I grow a little taller everyday.
Christmas is on the 25th December.
I always lose when I play a game.
Ice-cream melts in the sunshine.
I need water to live.
I wish I was taller.
I don't think I'm clever.
Earth is the third planet from the sun.
I feel sad sometimes.
I have a birthday every year.
Every dog will bite me.

Just a thought
A thought is an opinion that happens in our mind.

Definitely a fact
Facts are true statements.

Consider all the thoughts in your head. Now sort them into the correct box.

Just a thought
....
....
....
....
....
....

Definitely a fact
....
....
....
....
....
....

MINDFUL MAGIC
If you have lots of negative thoughts in your list, take a moment to use one of your tools to get rid of them.

Starfish Breathing

- Sit in a comfortable position.
- Place your right hand palm down, fingers spread wide like a starfish.
- Rest your left index finger lightly on the bottom of your right thumb.
- Trace up and down your thumb as you breathe in and out.
- Move to the next finger.
- Keep going until you've traced up and down each finger.
- You can repeat this on your other hand too!

MINDFUL MAGIC
This exercise can be practised anywhere, and is useful when you don't have much space.

Vision Board

Sometimes it's easier to show something visually than to express it in words. A vision board is a collage (collection of pictures) that represents all the good things in your life and things that make you happy, along with your goals and aspirations. It can be full of lots of different images, shapes, and textures. You can use your hippocampus to capture positive memories and inspirational ideas on the board.

If you want, you can cover the whole board with some wrapping paper or leftover wallpaper, or you can keep it plain.

Now let's decorate it with lots of things that inspire you. You'll have to go on a scavenger hunt to find the right things. They could include:

- Pictures from magazines
- Scraps of fabric
- Old birthday cards
- Photos
- Postcards
- Flowers
- Leaves
- Feathers

To make **your** Vision Board, **you** will need:

- A large piece of cardboard (the side of a cereal box is perfect)
- Glue or sticky tape

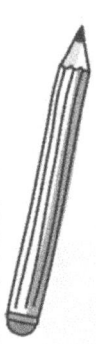

Use this space to plan your vision board.

Once you've gathered all the materials, stick them onto the board and hang it up in your room.

MINDFUL MAGIC
You can keep adding to this over time.

Take Flight

Make a paper plane and let your negative thoughts drift away, instead of spiralling into a tornado.

You will need:
- A4 paper
- A pen

How to:

1. Fold the paper in half lengthways.

2. Unfold and then fold the corners down into the middle line.

3. Fold the top edges to the middle.

4. Fold the plane in half.

5. Fold the wings down to meet the bottom edge of the planes body.

6. Write your thoughts on the plane and watch them fly away!

CONGRATULATIONS!

You've unlocked another three tools! These latest tools help you recognise your unwanted thoughts and build a stronger mind. Don't forget to keep a note of how many tools you have on the tracker at the end of this book.

In the Toolbox:

- Let your negative thoughts **Drift Away**.

- Create a **Vision Board** to focus on your goals.

- Count down to clarity with **Starfish Breathing**.

You are now ready to use these tools anywhere!

Chapter 3

Boost Your Confidence

In this chapter we're going to:

- Focus on things you can control
- Use the power of positivity to grow your mindset
- Be kind to yourself

Before we start, check in with yourself.

How confident are **you** as a person?

Mark your place on the scale
1 being not confident at all, and 10 being very confident.

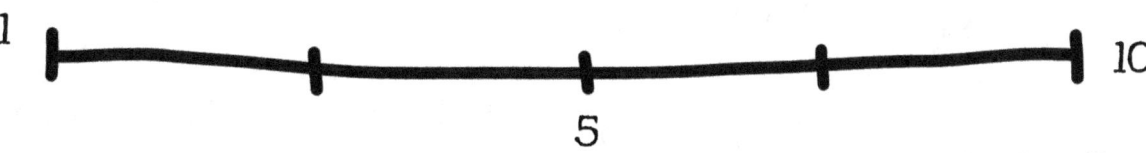

MINDFUL MAGIC

You are perfect as you are!

The Record Keeper

In this chapter we're going to train our hippocampus.

This part of the brain stores our short-term and long-term memories.

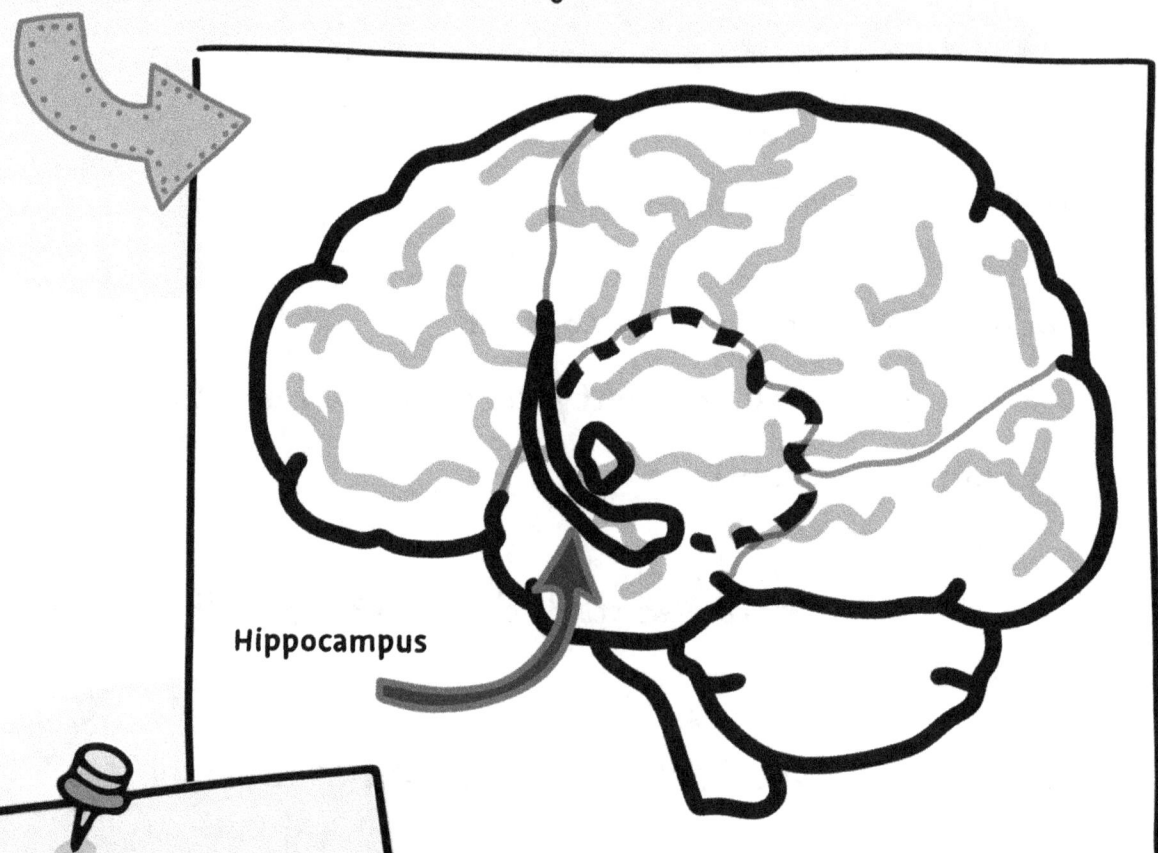

Hippocampus

The **hippocampus** uses your memory to help with your current activity.

For example, when you're doing homework, it helps you remember what you learned in class.

The **hippocampus** follows this formula:

Past experiences + Present tasks = Be your smartest self

COMPLIMENT CORNER

YOU ARE...

> Lots of people find it easier to compliment others rather than themselves.
>
> You have so many positive qualities!

calm
strong
helpful
positive
funny
generous
brave
curious
kind
thoughtful
considerate
sensitive
smart
trustworthy
friendly
smiley
ambitious
wonderful
clever
diligent
a good listener
intelligent
awesome
honest
empathetic
caring
1. Write it down
loveable
I AM _____
2. Say it!
warm-hearted
3. Believe it!
creative
unique

MINDFUL MAGIC

The more you say it, the more you will believe it. Try saying it to yourself in the morning when you wake up, during the day, before bed.

Business Card Boost

Design a business card for yourself!

- Put your name on this side and create your own logo or decorate it.
- Choose a quote below (or make up your own) for the other side.
- Keep it in your pencil case or phone case to look at when you need a boost.

* Positive Mind, Positive Life.
* I am the best version of myself.
* You've got to nourish yourself to flourish.
* Being happy never goes out of style.
* I AM ENOUGH.
* If you fall 7 times, stand up 8 times.
* I am not perfect but many parts of me are awesome!
* Life is tough, but so am I!
* Hope is stronger than Fear!
* If you're reading this, something great will happen to you today.

STRENGTH SHIELD

Picture a warrior tribe, and each warrior is carrying a shield.

You can build your own protective shield. In each section of the shield, make a list of the people who care about you and look out for you in each of these categories:

Categories:
People who **listen** to me.
People who can give me a **hug**.
People who can give me good **advice**.
People who make me **smile**.

This is your warrior tribe.
Now colour in your shield.

Listen · Hug · Advice · Smile

Decorate the back of your shield with your secret symbol. Nobody else will see it.

MINDFUL MAGIC

If it feels like you're alone, take a look at your tribe to see who's got your back (that means people who will support you). It's always OK to ask them for help.

Circle of Life

It's natural to want to control everything, but there are always going to be things we can't control. Lots of things. In fact, the things you **can** control are only a *piece of the puzzle*, of everything that goes on in your life.

When you learn to recognise the things you can't control and let them go, you can then focus your energy on the things you can control.

Can YOU add any other statements of things you CAN / CAN'T control?

Things I can control

- How I react to my feelings
- Who my friends are
- To be kind or not to be kind
- To work hard in school
- ....
- ....
- ....
- ....

Things I can't control

- Weather
- Day and night
- Getting older
- Who my family are
- Traffic lights
- Feelings
- ....
- ....
- ....
- ....
- ....

Decisions Decisions

If you can't decide what to do to make yourself smile, let this decision wheel help.

MAKING YOUR DECISION WHEEL:

1. Colour in the wheel.

2. Cut out the hexagon and stick it to a piece of cardboard to make it stronger.

3. Push the split pin or matchstick through the middle.

You will need:

- cardboard
- pencils/pens
- scissors
- a cocktail stick

USING YOUR DECISION WHEEL:

1. Hold the cocktail stick between your finger and thumb and spin it.

2. Read the decision it has revealed and do it.

3. Have fun!

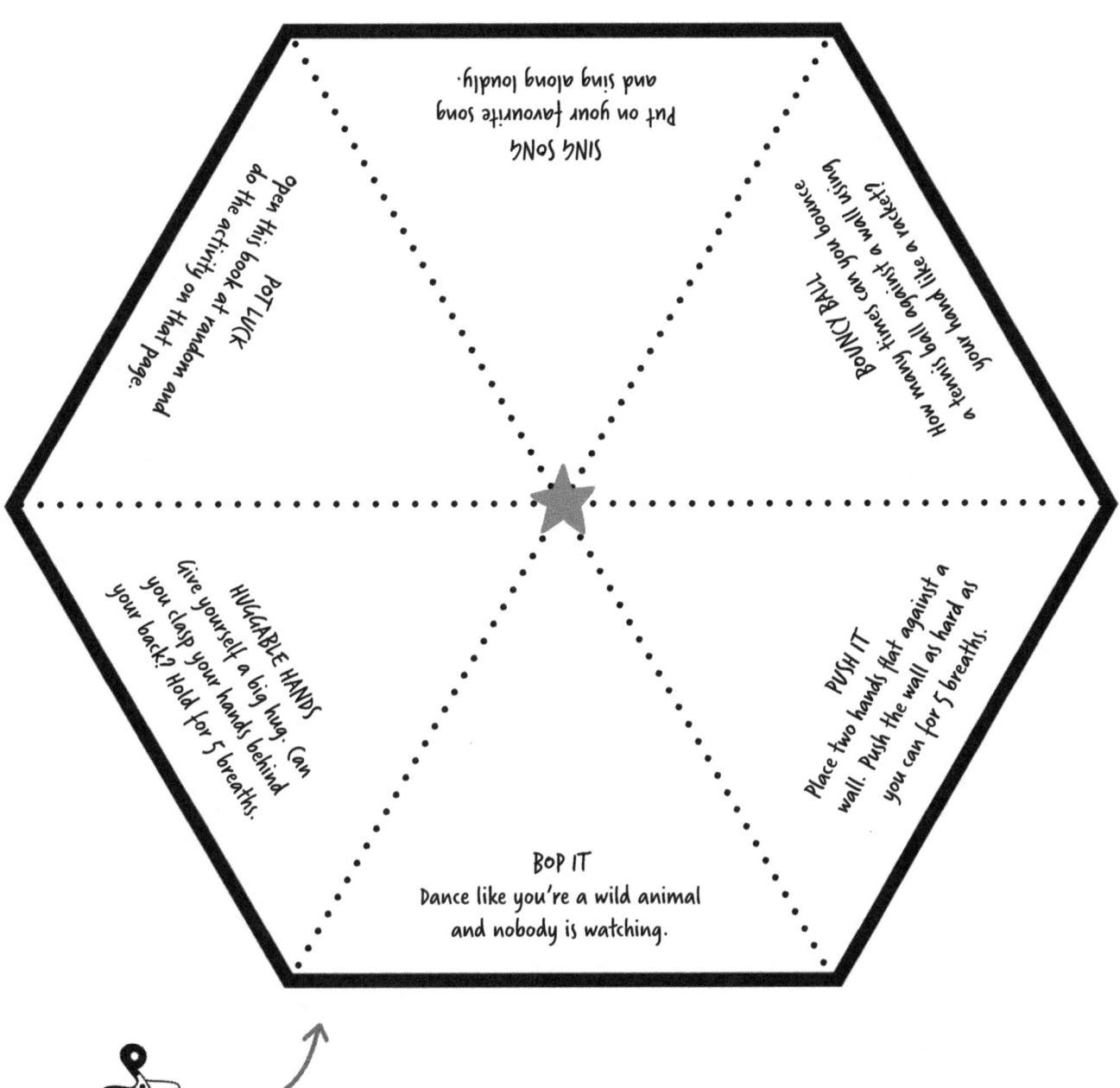

HELP
I CAN'T DECIDE!

ANCHORED BREATHING

Before you begin this exercise, you need to make an anchor.

YOU WILL NEED:

* an old but clean pair of socks
* 250g of rice (uncooked)
* two pieces of string, each one about 30 cm long
* (optional) a funnel

How to:

1. Carefully pour the rice into one of the socks (you can use a funnel if you have one).
2. Use your string to tie the top of the sock closed.
3. Place the other sock over the top and tie it closed as well.

- Find a place where you won't get disturbed.
- Stand with your feet shoulder width apart.
- Place your sock "anchor" on top of your feet.
- Visualise your body as a ship in the water and your feet anchored to the seabed.
- Breathe in and smell the fresh ocean air. Listen to the waves.
- Breathe out and make a 'shhhhhhh' sound through your mouth.
- Rock backwards and forwards. Sway from side to side.
- See how far can you move before the anchor starts to pull away from the seabed.
- Begin to bring yourself back to a balanced, still place.
- Wriggle your toes into the sandy seabed.

Say to yourself "I am anchored and I am happy being me."

MINDFUL MAGIC

Try standing on top of your anchor. How do you feel balancing on it instead?

CONGRATULATIONS!

You have unlocked yet another three mindfulness tools! The tools from this chapter help you to nurture yourself and boost your confidence by understanding that you have control over your own emotions.

In the Toolbox:

 Check your **Business Card** for a positive boost.

 Hold up your **Strength Shield** when you want to find support.

 Keep yourself grounded with **Anchored Breathing**.

You are now ready to use these tools anywhere!

Chapter 4

Identify your Emotions

In this chapter we're going to:

- Recognise different emotions
- Explore how colour and emotions are connected
- Discover the power of a simple smile

Before we start, check in with yourself.

Where are you right now? Draw yourself on the hill.

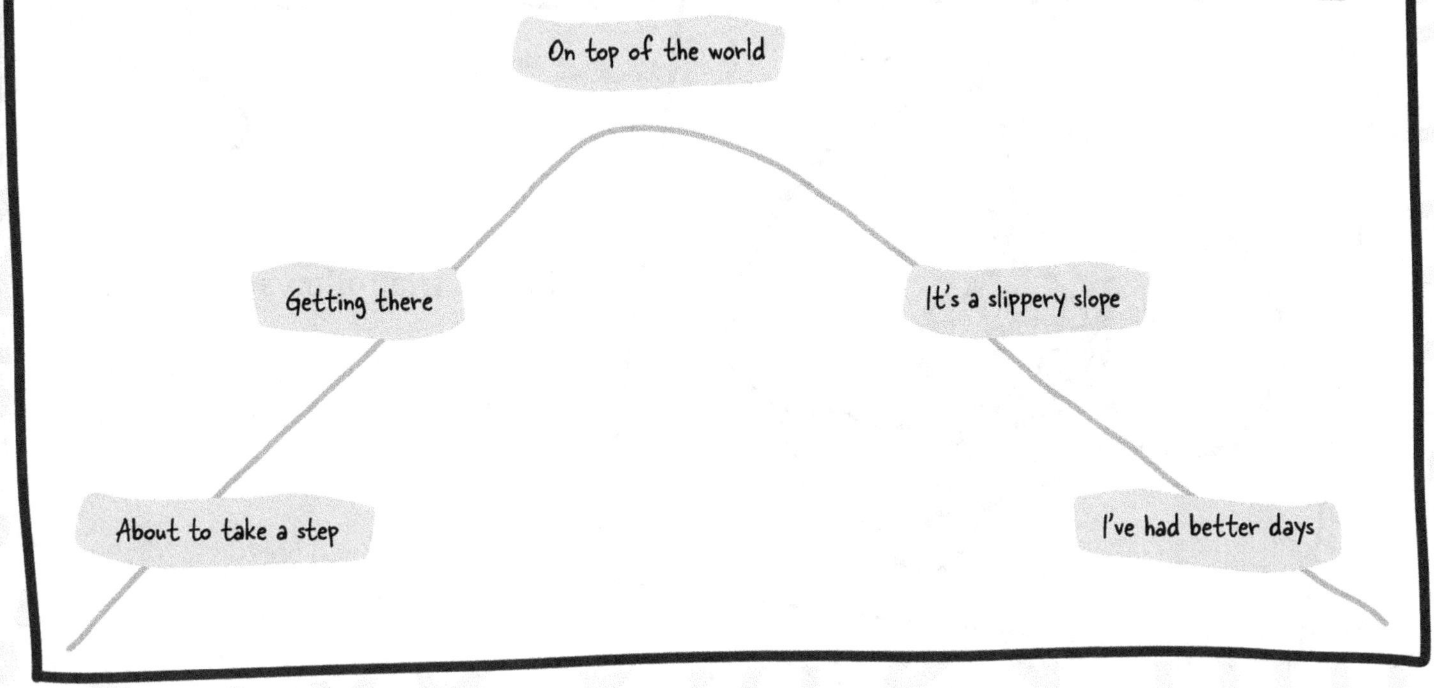

On top of the world

Getting there

It's a slippery slope

About to take a step

I've had better days

The Emotions Radar

If you're working through this book in order, you'll already have seen how

- The focus function (prefrontal cortex) helps us to make smart choices.
- The record keeper (hippocampus) helps us to learn from our experiences.

Now we're going to look at the third part of the brain.

The INSULA

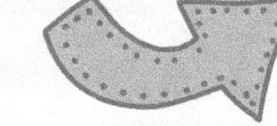

The insula provides empathy and helps you understand feelings. For example, if you can't sit still because you're about to go to a party, it recognises you're excited!

It can also help you recognise other people's feelings. For example, your friend may begin to cry if you hurt their feelings by not playing with them or laughing at them. Your insula helps you understand how they're feeling.

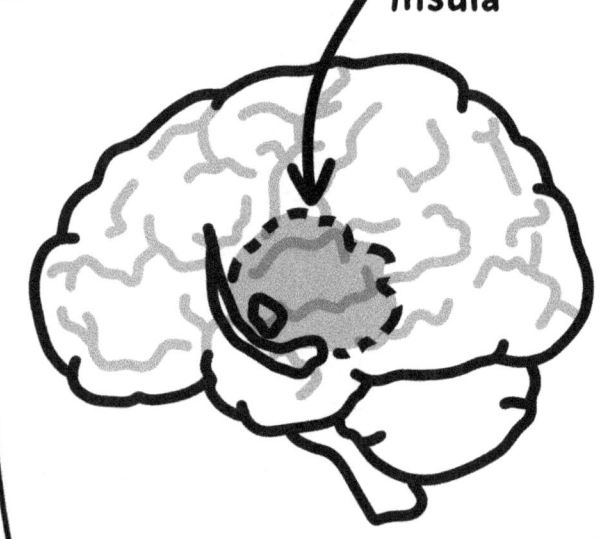

Insula

The insula follows this formula:

Understand your own emotions + Recognise how others feel = Be your most caring self

Emotion Doodle

Think about what colour best represents the mood you are in now. Maybe you have 2 colours that you are feeling throughout this exercise?

Take your coloured pencil for a wander around the page and see what words, pictures, and/ or doodles you make using your colour.

My Colours:

Can you describe your emotion?

My colour is _____ because I feel _____
_____.

The Colour of Calm

1. Find a safe and quiet space.
2. Sit in a comfortable position.
3. Picture a calm colour.
4. Now close your eyes.
5. Take three deep breaths in through your nose and out through your mouth.
6. Imagine that colour as a light flowing into you.
7. Let your mind and body fill up with that colour.
8. Open your eyes and say:

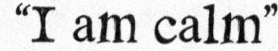
"I am calm"

GLITTER GLOBE

Make a glitter globe to shake away unwanted emotions or sensations.

How to make your glitter globe:

1. Pour the warm water into the jar.
2. Add in the glitter.
3. Add in the PVA/ glitter glue.
4. Stir the mixture round.
5. If you have food colouring add in a few drops.
6. Put the lid on tightly.

YOU WILL NEED:

- a recycled clean glass jar (*Top tip: it looks nice if you can remove any labels)
- a LOT of glitter
- enough warm water to ¾ fill the jar
- a tablespoon of PVA glue or glitter glue
- optional: food colouring

How to use your glitter globe:

- Shake the jar then put it down on a flat surface.
- Place your hands out in front of you, either on a table or on your knee, palms facing down.
- Focus on each piece of glitter as it rises and falls.
- Take gentle breaths in and out through your nose watching the glitter settle.
- Feel your mind slowing down along with the glitter.
- Stay focused on the pieces of glitter until every piece comes to rest.
- Say out loud to yourself **"I am calm and peaceful"**.

 Like a multi-coloured rainbow, every day we have a range of emotions. By acknowledging these feelings, for example during a difficult lesson or an exciting sports match, we can use our toolkit to help ourselves to feel calmer.

Over the Rainbow

I felt angry when ...

I felt worried when ...

I felt tired when ...

I felt shy when ...

I felt calm when ...

I felt excited when ...

I felt energetic when ...

MINDFUL MAGIC
Try using the Colour of Calm breathing tool from the previous page to get rid of those negative thoughts.

Well done for acknowledging all your feelings!

Try and focus on the positive ones.

3... 2... 1...

Smile Happy

The insula recognises emotions by analysing facial expressions and body language. Did you know that a simple smile encourages your insula to think positively?

What do you notice about how you feel inside when you smile at people?
....
....

Did people smile back?
....
....

YOUR CHALLENGE

Smile at everybody today!

Roar Like a Lion

Like a lion roaring or a cat yawning, you can use your breath to release any extra energy or tension in your body.

Take a deep breath in through the nose.

Open your mouth wide.

AND ROAR.

...ROAR!

CONGRATULATIONS!

That's another set of mindfulness tools in your toolbox! These new tools help you to reconnect your body and mind, and become more aware of when your feelings change. Have you added up how many tools you now have?

In the Toolbox:

 Surround yourself with the **Colour of Calm**.

 Settle your emotions with the **Glitter Globe**.

 Let it all out with a **Lion Roar**.

You are now ready to use these tools anywhere!

Chapter 5

Master Your Instincts

In this chapter we're going to:

- Learn to tame your thoughts.
- Understand fight, flight, and freeze reactions.
- Analyse your response before acting.

Before we start, check in with yourself.

How do you feel right now?

....
....

Imagine your feelings are sitting on the other side of the scales. Is it balanced or tipped in one direction?

Draw your scales here.

MINDFUL MAGIC
Don't worry if your scales are uneven. The activities in this book can help you balance them.

The Survival Instinct

If you're working through this book in order, you'll know

- The focus function (pre frontal cortex) helps us make smart choices.
- The record keeper (hippocampus) helps us learn from our experiences.
- The emotions radar (insula) helps us be kind and caring.

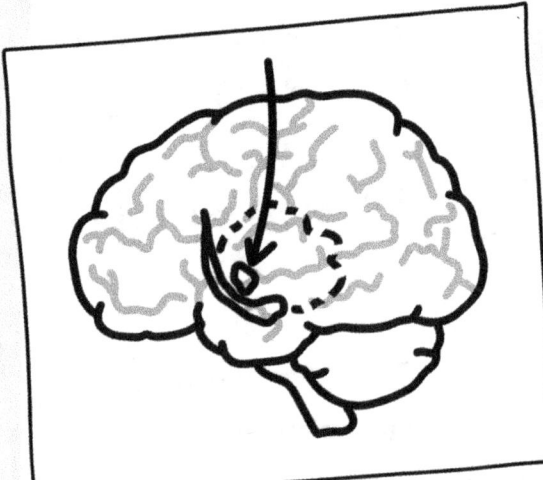

There is one last part of the brain that is important when you are practising mindfulness. The **amygdala**. It may be small, but it is mighty! It evaluates if something is a threat or not.

The amygdala follows the formula:

Pause your instinct + Process the situation = Choose your reaction

Animals have one of three survival instincts:

Fight. Flight. Freeze

Animals rely on their dominant instinct to help them survive.

Connect these animals to their instinct, the first one has been done for you.

Rabbit — Fight
Horse — Flight
Cheetah — Freeze

Fight = 'attack'

Flight = 'run away'

Freeze = 'stay still'

HUMAN REACTIONS

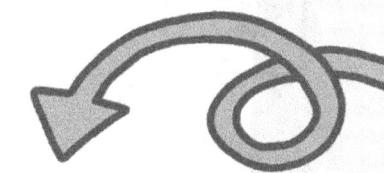

Whilst animals only have one pre-programmed response, humans have all three of these instincts. This is really cool, as it means we can choose how to react.

Can you match the scenarios to the reaction?

(Hint: there are two situations to be matched to each reaction.)

MINDFUL MAGIC

Sometimes, it can be helpful to consider the best response before we react. We can train our brain to think before we react by practising mindfulness.

"The world we have created is a product of our thinking; it cannot be changed without changing our thinking."

—Albert Einstein

ANIMAL TAMER

1 Next time you want to do or say something bad, write it down instead.

2 Say out loud, "This is just a thought. It is not a FACT. I will not think about it again." Cross the thought out.

3 Now think of something you could say or do instead. Depending on where you are/ the time of day etc, these will be different.

- Read a book?
- Do my homework?
- Talk to a friend?
- Play football?
- Tidy your room?

MINDFUL MAGIC

Sometimes thoughts are like rampaging elephants. By practising mindfulness, you can help yourself recognise this and stop the elephant from destroying everything!

EMOTION CHARADES

Play this game with a friend or your family.

Can they guess the scenario AND how you feel?

-RULES-

* Choose a scenario from the list, or make up your own.

* Act it out.

* You can't talk or make any sounds!

Losing a game
Forgetting your homework
Eating cold peas
Squishing a snail
Getting told off at school
Scoring a goal
Winning an award at school
Taking an exam
Riding a rollercoaster
Falling asleep in class
Losing your mobile phone
Playing with your friends in the park
Being kept in at lunchtime
Performing in front of the school

MINDFUL MAGIC
Try to show the FLIGHT FIGHT FREEZE reaction to the scenario.

CAT CURL

1. Find a comfortable space.
2. Place your hands and knees on the floor. Make sure your hands are under your shoulders, and your knees under your hips, with the soles of your feet facing upwards.
3. Take a deep breath in and arch your back upwards towards the sky.
4. Let your breath out through your mouth as you push your back towards the ground into a concave position.
5. Repeat this five times.
6. Return to a kneeling position.
7. Take a deep breath in through your nose.
8. Breathe out and let your body relax.
9. Say out loud, "I am calm and peaceful".

INSTINCT INTERPRETER

Think about how your body feels when your amygdala is telling you which instinct to follow.
- Can you match these feelings to the likely reaction?

FLIGHT
Run away from the situation.

FIGHT
Attack the situation.

heart racing
sweaty palms
shaky legs
tingly
sick
breathing hard

FREEZE
'Stand still'.

MINDFUL MAGIC
There is no right or wrong answer. We are all human and react in different ways.

A SQUASH AND A SQUEEZE

You will need:

* 2 Balloons
* Elastic band
* Bag of flour (500g approx.)
* Funnel
* Scissors

To decorate:

* Felt tip marker pen
* Googly eyes
* 'Hair' e.g. string or wool or pipe cleaners cut into about 5cm pieces

MINDFUL MAGIC

Before reacting to a situation, play with the squisher while you consider if it's your animal instinct taking over and if you should **choose** another response.

How to make a squish ball:

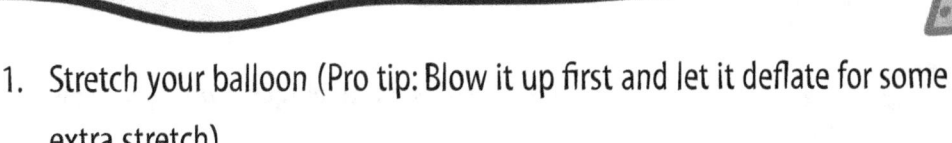

1. Stretch your balloon (Pro tip: Blow it up first and let it deflate for some extra stretch).

2. Stick a funnel into the neck of the balloon.

3. Slowly fill the balloon with flour.

4. Remove the funnel from the balloon and gently squeeze out as much air as you can. Try not to blow flour all over the room!

5. Take your hair (if using) and slide it into the neck of the balloon. Hold them tightly.

6. Take the second balloon and pull it over the filled first balloon so it creates a thicker layer over the first balloon. This can be a bit tricky!

7. Use the elastic band to tie the neck leaving the 'hair' sticking out.

8. Decorate the ball. You could make a face using googly eyes or a pen.

CONGRATULATIONS!

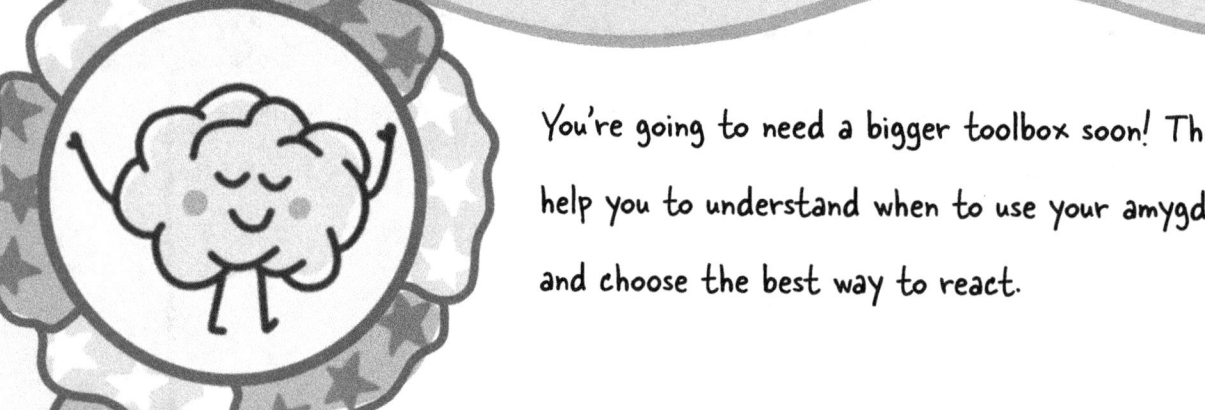

You're going to need a bigger toolbox soon! These latest tools help you to understand when to use your amygdala in daily life and choose the best way to react.

In the Toolbox:

- Be an **Animal Tamer** and control your unwanted thoughts.

- Use your physical reaction to **Interpret your Instincts**.

- **Cat Curl** away any unwanted sensations.

You are now ready to use these tools anywhere!

Chapter 6

Read Your Weather Forecast

In this chapter we're going to:

- Notice how your emotions can change like the weather
- Recognise that clouds do go away
- Try changing your emotional "weather"

Before we start, check in with yourself.

Draw your facial expression in the mirror reflecting how you feel right now.

THE BIG BRAIN TEST

When all parts of the brain work together, we can be our best self!

1. How many times have you used your memory (hippocampus) today?

- ☐ 1-10 times
- ☐ 10-20 times
- ☐ >20 times

2. Have you used your insula today to notice someone's feelings?

- ☐ Yes. That's great!
- ☐ No. Don't worry. Try to use it tomorrow.

3. Did you notice when you used the prefrontal cortex to help you concentrate today?

Yes
- ☐ At school?
- ☐ At home?
- ☐ At the Park?
- ☐ Somewhere else?
  _____

No
That's ok! See if you notice it tomorrow.

4. Which survival instincts did you tame with your amygdala this week?

- ☐ Fight
- ☐ Flight
- ☐ Freeze

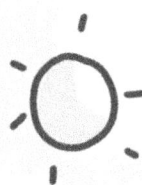

Weather Wordsearch

G	E	T	W	K	V	B	D	F	R	Z	L	Y	R	G
W	N	A	E	F	Z	R	N	B	N	F	I	K	E	N
G	H	I	R	M	I	C	A	O	D	F	G	D	H	I
T	O	O	Z	Z	P	R	Y	H	O	Y	H	U	T	W
H	S	G	Z	E	O	E	S	C	O	S	T	T	A	O
T	U	L	S	M	E	C	R	V	L	R	N	U	E	N
U	E	D	E	U	L	R	S	A	L	O	I	O	W	S
D	F	T	N	L	A	S	F	T	T	E	N	S	M	B
O	E	N	A	C	I	R	R	U	H	U	G	E	W	T
R	J	U	C	L	O	U	D	S	D	K	R	O	S	O
N	Q	T	H	U	N	D	E	R	U	N	B	E	T	R
S	E	N	I	A	R	F	V	A	V	N	I	U	O	N
O	L	T	H	G	U	O	R	D	I	P	N	W	R	A
X	A	F	O	G	K	P	F	A	H	W	T	Y	M	D
J	G	H	R	X	M	K	R	E	H	X	O	A	G	O

BAROMETER	FREEZING	RAIN	TEMPERATURE
CLOUD	FROST	RAINBOW	THAW
CYCLONE	GALE	SNOWING	THUNDER
DRIZZLE	HURRICANE	SQUALL	TORNADO
DROUGHT	LIGHTNING	STORM	WEATHER
FOG	MONSOON	SUNNY	WIND

# Wonderful Weather Mobile

You will need:

* Two twigs about 30 cm long

* 1 pipe cleaner or craft wire

* Four pieces of coloured ribbon or yarn of different lengths from 15cm to 30cm

* 60cm plain string

* Cardboard (optional)

* Scissors

* Glue or stapler

* Colouring pencils/ pens or paints or glitter

Instructions:

1. Put the two sticks in a cross shape and use the pipe cleaner or craft wire to tie them together.
2. Cut out the four weather symbols and colour them in.
3. Stick your symbols onto the cardboard (if using) and cut round the shapes. This just makes your mobile stronger.
4. Glue or staple the weather symbols to the different coloured ribbons and tie them onto the ends of the sticks.
5. Now use the long piece of string to hang your weather mobile up.

cut carefully around the sun,
it looks hot!

Windscreen Wipers

Begin by finding a quiet, comfortable place. Maybe it's where you are right now?

Picture yourself sitting inside a car on a rainy day.

Visualise all your unwanted emotions as the raindrops on the windscreen.

Watch the windscreen wipers swish the raindrops away.

Imagine the wipers sweeping away all your unwanted emotions.

Take a deep breath in.

Let it out.

Keep wiping away all the unwanted emotions until your windscreen is clear.

MINDFUL MAGIC

As an alternative, try picturing yourself going through a car wash. Which image works better for you?

WEATHER REPORT

Match the weather report to how it makes you feel.

WILD   TIRED   HAPPY   ANGRY   CALM   UPSET

Keep a record of your emotional weather for a week. Today the weather was...

MONDAY

TUESDAY

WEDNESDAY

THURSDAY

FRIDAY

SATURDAY

SUNDAY

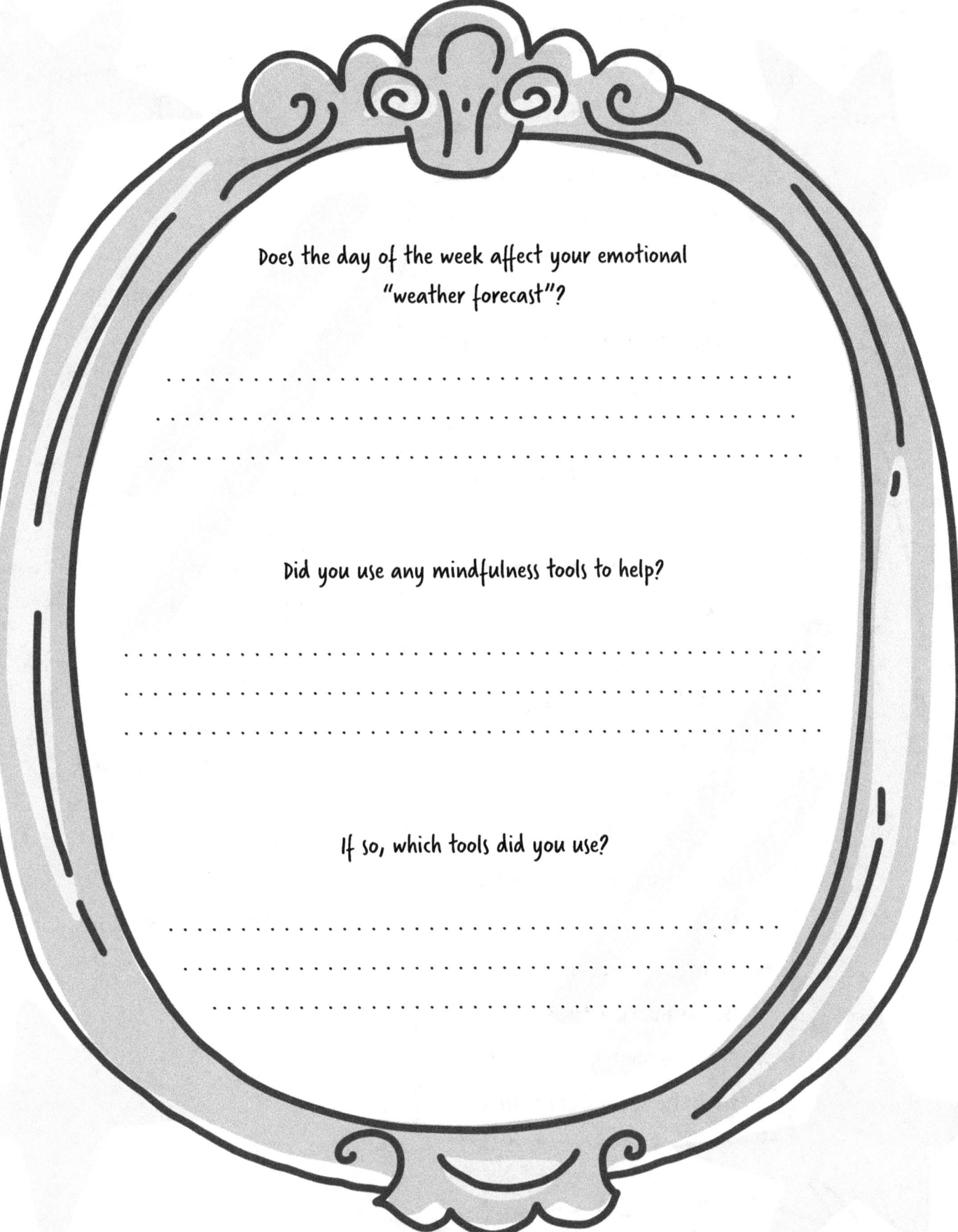

Does the day of the week affect your emotional "weather forecast"?

....
....
....

Did you use any mindfulness tools to help?

....
....
....

If so, which tools did you use?

....
....
....

RAIN STICK

INSTRUCTIONS:

1. Trace round the tube onto the cardboard to make two circles for end caps. Cut them out.
2. Seal one end of the tube with one of the card circles. Secure it with tape.
3. Decorate the tube however you like.
4. Roll the strips of tin foil into three long sausage-like shapes.
5. Very loosely plait the three pieces of tin foil together and place the plait inside the tube.
6. Pour the cup of rice/ beans/ lentils into the tube.
7. Seal the open end of the tube with the second card circle.

YOU WILL NEED:

- Cup of uncooked rice/ dried lentils or beans
- A 30cm long cardboard tube roll e.g. from gift wrapping paper, a paper towel roll, or a postage tube
- A4 card / cardboard
- Scissors
- Sticky tape
- Three strips of tinfoil approx. 30cm long by 10cm wide
- Anything to decorate the tube – washi tape, wrapping paper, paint, ribbons ….

Close your eyes and slowly turn the rain stick upside down. Listen to the sound of the grains as they fall through the stick. Imagine the sound of rain drops falling on leaves in a rainforest.

MINDFUL MAGIC

When you want to help refocus, turn your rainstick over several times and let the soft rainfall sounds clear your mind. That's you controlling your amygdala!

Cloud Breathing

- Find a calm and quiet place to sit down.

- Sit with your legs crossed or on a chair.

- Imagine you are at the top of a mountain and surrounded only by light fluffy clouds.

- Now close your eyes.

- Place your hands on your belly.

- Begin to notice your belly rising and falling as you breathe.

- Count each time your belly rises until you get to 10.

- Every time you breathe out, imagine you are blowing away the clouds surrounding you until you see a clear blue sky and sunshine.

- Then focus on counting each time your belly falls until you get to 10.

How do you feel now?
....
....

THUNDER BUSTER

Write or draw all your negative feelings on this thunder cloud. Tear out the page, rip it into tiny pieces, and throw them away.

Rip me up! It won't hurt me, I promise.

CONGRATULATIONS!

Your toolbox is really full now! The new tools from this chapter help to lift your mood.

In the Toolbox:

 Switch on your **Windscreen Wipers** to swish any raindrops away.

 Blast through any negative feelings with the **Thunder Buster**.

 Use the power of your breathing to blow away those **Clouds**.

You are now ready to use these tools anywhere!

Chapter 7

Pay it Forward

In this chapter we're going to:

- show compassion to yourself and others
- spread kindness everywhere you go
- Be grateful for who you are and what you have

Before we start, check in with yourself and notice how you are feeling right now.

Start by closing your eyes. Picture a flower.

- What colour is it?
- What shape are its petals?
- How does it smell?

Now open your eyes and draw it on this page:

MASTER YOUR MIND

When the cogs in your brain work together, you can be your best self.

Colour in the part of the brain that helps you to notice feelings.

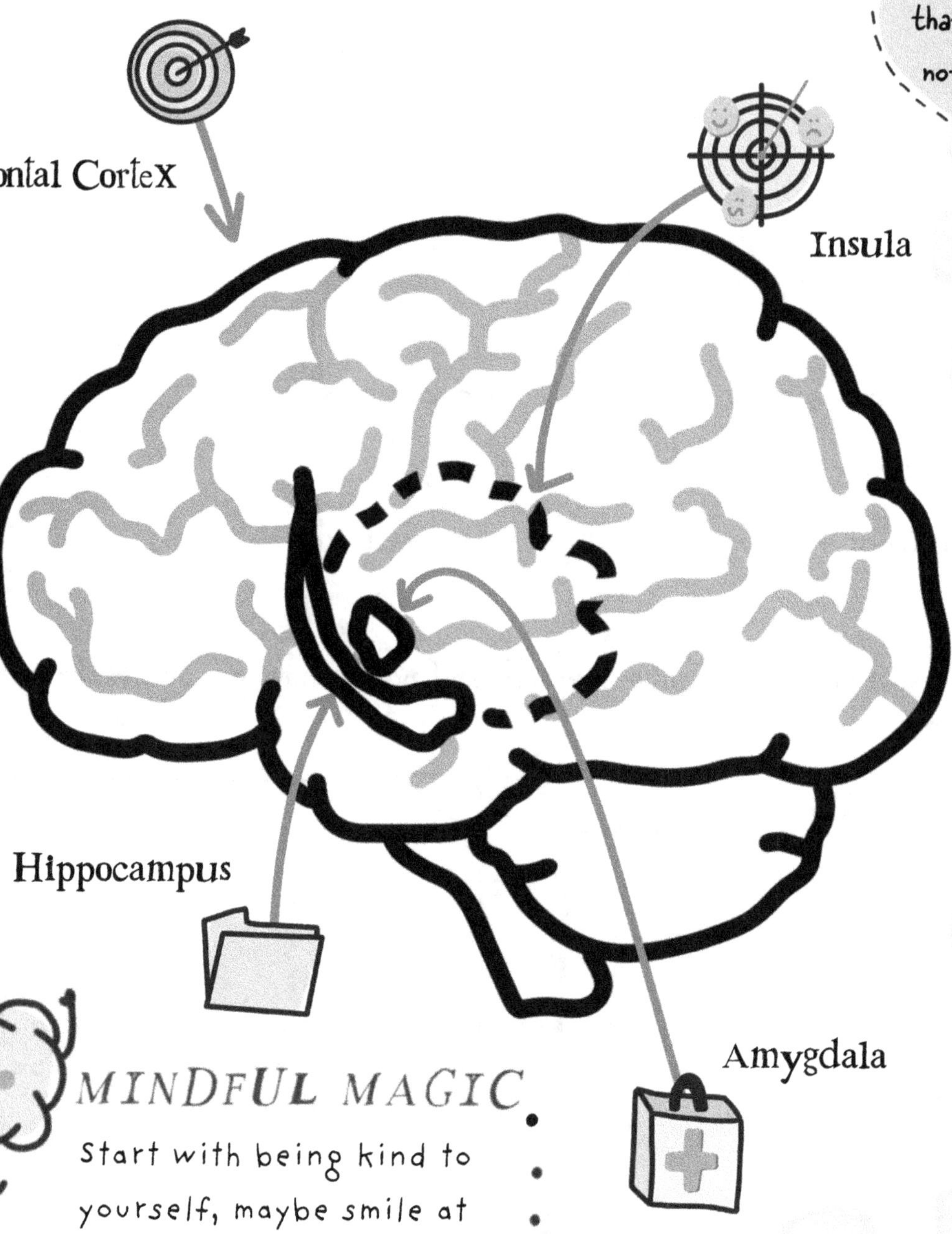

Pre frontal Cortex

Insula

Hippocampus

Amygdala

MINDFUL MAGIC

Start with being kind to yourself, maybe smile at yourself in the mirror or do an activity you love like drawing or singing. How does it make you feel?

Tree Me

There's no right or wrong answer!

What Tree are You Most Like?

A generous fruit tree? A brave fir tree? A strong oak tree? Another kind of tree?

Draw a picture of your tree.

Hugs for Heroes

You can boost your happiness by giving yourself a hug.
Whenever you notice your insula reacting to unwanted feelings you can use this tool.

1. Begin by sitting in a comfortable position, either on the floor or on a chair.

2. Spread your fingers wide and stretch your arms out to the sides.

3. Wrap your arms around your body and try to touch your fingers behind your back.

4. Hold for three breaths in and three breaths out.

5. Now, release and stretch your body.

How do you feel now?

....

....

....

Showing kindness helps spread happiness

MINDFUL MAGIC
Share this activity with anybody you think needs a hug.

COPING WITH CHANGE

Things change all the time. Sometimes these are big changes (like moving house), sometimes they're small (like it starts to rain).

Change can make anyone feel uneasy, maybe confused and sometimes a feeling you are not sure about. The first step to taking control of the new situation is to acknowledge the change.

MINDFUL MAGIC

Try making little changes in your life, like rearranging your room, or taking a different route to school, so that you can get used to the feeling of things being different.

Make a list of things that have changed inside your house:

1.
2.
3.
4.
5.

Now think about things that have changed at school:

1.
2.
3.
4.
5.

What other changes have there been in your life?

1.
2.
3.
4.
5.

Butterfly Box

Challenge yourself to do something kind every day for a month.
You can use these butterflies as prompts for your acts of kindness, or make up your own.

To make your butterfly box you will need:

- An empty box with a lid (e.g. shoe box/ washing tablet box)
- Your favourite colour pens and paint
- Card / tissue paper / wrapping paper
- Glue
- Optional: sequins / glitter / stickers for decoration

Decorate the box any way you like!

Cut out the butterflies and put them into your Kindness Box. Every morning, pick one out at random and complete your challenge!

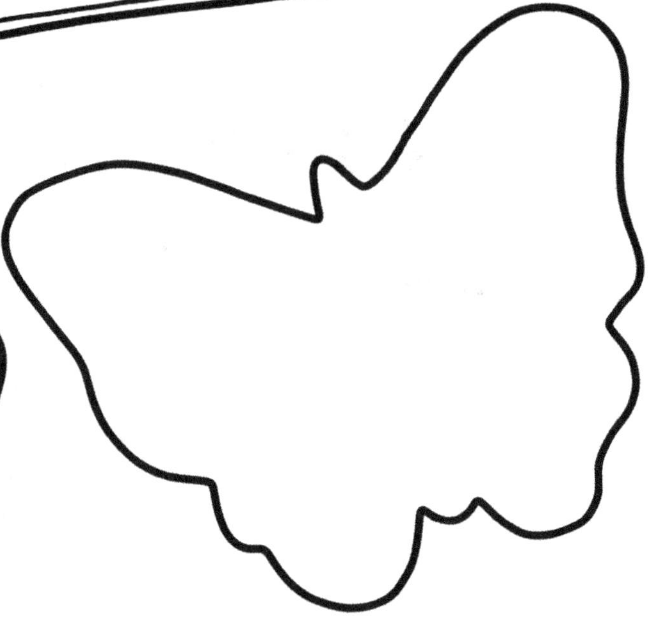

You can use these as templates or draw your own butterflies.

Here are some ideas for things you could do.

- Make your bed
- Help put the dishes away
- Phone a relative
- Donate one of your toys to charity
- Pick up litter (wear gloves to do this)
- Put your dirty clothes in the laundry
- Write a thank you letter
- Smile at everyone you see today
- Help prepare dinner
- Set the table
- Help fold the clean clothes
- Hold a door open for someone
- Give someone a gift you've made
- Feed the birds
- Give your friend a hug
- Play with someone different

- Help tidy the classroom
- Share your snacks with someone
- Give someone a compliment
- Clear the table after eating
- Draw a portrait of someone and give it to them
- Tell your parent / sibling you love them
- Eat lunch with someone different today
- Help someone with their studies
- Read a story to someone
- Tidy your bedroom
- Donate some old clothes to charity
- Ask someone what you could do to help them
- Carry someone's bag
- Talk to someone who looks sad
- Learn to say "hello" in a different language

POCKET HUGS

Cut out these hearts and colour them in.
Keep them in your pocket and give one to a friend when they need cheering up.

CONGRATULATIONS!

Wow! You have just unlocked the final three mindfulness tools for this book! These will help you to show kindness both to yourself and to others.

In the Toolbox:

 Schedule weekly 'gratitude' tasks from your **Butterfly Box**.

 Keep a stash of **Pocket Hugs** with you.

 Plan time for **Hugs for Heroes**.

You are now ready to use these tools anywhere!

INDEX

All the activities in this book can be repeated, tick the ones you have tried.

Breathing
- [ ] Be a Tree
- [ ] Starfish Breathing
- [ ] Anchored Breathing
- [ ] Roar like a Lion
- [ ] Cat Curl
- [ ] Cloud Breathing
- [ ] Hugs for Heroes

Visualisation
- [ ] Wave Rider
- [ ] Drift Away
- [ ] Strength Shield
- [ ] Colour of Calm
- [ ] Animal Tamer
- [ ] Windscreen Wiper
- [ ] Tree Me

Games
- [ ] Confidence Cube
- [ ] Take Flight
- [ ] Decisions Decisions
- [ ] Glitter Globe
- [ ] Emotions Charades
- [ ] Weather Wordsearch
- [ ] Butterfly Box

Analysis
- [ ] Activity See-saw
- [ ] Fact or Fiction Sorter
- [ ] Circle of Life
- [ ] Over the Rainbow
- [ ] Instinct Interpreter
- [ ] Weather Report
- [ ] Coping with Change

To do
- [ ] Worry Jar
- [ ] Vision Board
- [ ] Compliment Corner
- [ ] Smile Happy
- [ ] A Squash and a Squeeze
- [ ] Rain Stick
- [ ] Thunder Buster
- [ ] Pocket Hugs

Art
- [ ] Best Self Statement
- [ ] Waves of Positivity
- [ ] Business Card Boost
- [ ] Emotion Doodle
- [ ] Einstein Quote
- [ ] Wonderful Weather Mobile
- [ ] Nature Doodle

Notes

BE MORE YOU

SASHA MULLEN

Sasha has always had a passion for adventure. Be it experiencing the sights, sounds and smells of far flung continents to exploring her hometown of West London. Letting her senses guide her head or heart, she has utilised her personal experiences to gather a kaleidoscope of skills. How to embrace a teaching role in New York- a city so vast and vibrant, how to cope with grief, transition into motherhood. Being a teacher in primary schools since 2010 has enabled her to see the need for incorporating Mindfulness practice into everyday education. When Sasha is not teaching or enjoying her family or socialising with friends, she is taking an exercise class, and is particularly fond of the child's pose in yoga, when she can happily have a power snooze!

 themindfulmentors.com   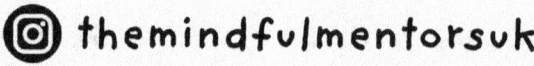 themindfulmentorsuk

LEXI REES

Lexi was born in Edinburgh and grew up in the Scottish Highlands, although she now lives down south. When she's not writing or tutoring, she's a keen crafter and spends a considerable amount of time trying not to fall off horses or boats. She's usually covered in sand, straw, or glitter.

🏠 lexirees.co.uk   📷 lexi.rees

Also by the Authors

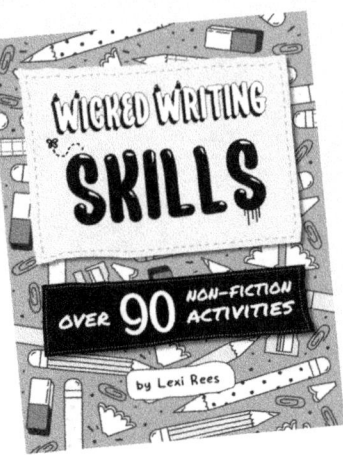

www.ingramcontent.com/pod-product-compliance
Lightning Source LLC
Chambersburg PA
CBHW081338080526
44588CB00017B/2661